T0014389

What's the Issue?

WHAT'S LAW AND ORDER?

By Amy Holt

KidHaven
PUBLISHING

Published in 2022 by
KidHaven Publishing, an Imprint of Greenhaven Publishing, LLC
353 3rd Avenue
Suite 255
New York, NY 10010

Copyright © 2022 KidHaven Publishing, an Imprint of Greenhaven Publishing, LLC.

All rights reserved. No part of this book may be reproduced in any form without permission in writing from the publisher, except by a reviewer.

Designer: Deanna Paternostro
Editor: Jennifer Lombardo

Photo credits: Cover (top) everything possible/Shutterstock.com; cover (bottom) SDI Productions/E+/Getty Images; p. 5 rubberball/Brand X Pictures/Getty Images; p. 7 Vera Petrunina/Shutterstock.com; p. 9 (top) Courtesy of the Library of Congress; p. 9 (bottom) Don Carl Steffen/Gamma-Rapho via Getty Images; p. 11 John Moore/Getty Images; p. 13 PixMarket/Shutterstock.com; p. 15 (main) a katz/Shutterstock.com; p. 15 (inset) Nic Neufeld/Shutterstock.com; p. 17 (main) LightField Studios/Shutterstock.com; p. 17 (inset) Fotosenmeer/Shutterstock.com; p. 19 Manuela Durson/Shutterstock.com; p. 21 Sylfida/Shutterstock.com.

Cataloging-in-Publication Data

Names: Holt, Amy.
Title: What's law and order?/ Amy Holt.
Description: New York : KidHaven Publishing, 2022. | Series: What's the issue? | Includes glossary and index.
Identifiers: ISBN 9781534534520 (pbk.) | ISBN 9781534534544 (library bound) | ISBN 9781534534537 (6 pack) | ISBN 9781534534551 (ebook)
Subjects: LCSH: Law enforcement–Juvenile literature. | Criminal justice, Administration of–Juvenile literature.
Classification: LCC HV7922.H65 2022 | DDC 363.2–dc23

Printed in the United States of America

Some of the images in this book illustrate individuals who are models. The depictions do not imply actual situations or events.

CPSIA compliance information: Batch #CS22KH: For further information contact Greenhaven Publishing LLC, New York, New York at 1-844-317-7404.

Please visit our website, www.greenhavenpublishing.com. For a free color catalog of all our high-quality books, call toll free 1-844-317-7404 or fax 1-844-317-7405.

Find us on

CONTENTS

Tough on Crime

People who say they support "law and order" generally want criminals, or people who **commit** crimes, to be **punished**. These people also sometimes say they're "**tough** on crime."

The criminal justice system is an important part of keeping law and order. This system includes the police, judges, the president, and other people who make and **enforce** the laws of a country. However, "law and order" can be confusing because not everyone agrees on exactly what this idea means. Some people say it's always a good thing to support. Others believe it's sometimes used to argue for ideas that can be harmful.

Facing the Facts

The crime rate helps people see how much crime there is in an area. To find the crime rate, they divide the number of crimes by the number of people who live in that area. Then, they multiply that number by 100,000.

The law is very **complicated**. That's why some people go to school for years to learn how it works and how to explain it to others. These people are called lawyers.

Understanding the Law

When people talk about "the law," they're talking about the system of rules that keep a country or community safe and fair. Each of those rules is also called a law.

There are a lot of different punishments for breaking the law. It depends on which law a person breaks. If it's a **minor** law, they might have to pay a fine. If it's a major law, they might go to jail. Laws are important because they're how we keep order. Without them, people wouldn't be punished for anything they did wrong—even if they hurt someone else.

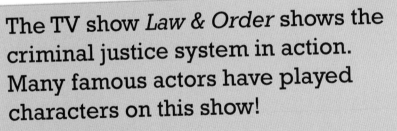

Facing the Facts

The TV show *Law & Order* shows the criminal justice system in action. Many famous actors have played characters on this show!

Speeding is against the law because it's unsafe. When someone drives too fast, they often can't stop in time to avoid hitting someone or something.

Keeping Order

There are many people who enforce laws. Some people, such as sheriffs, mayors, and police officers, enforce the law in towns or cities. The president and vice president, who lead the executive branch of the U.S. government, enforce the law for the whole country.

When Donald Trump ran for U.S. president in 2016, he called himself "the law-and-order **candidate**." He wanted people to know that he cared about enforcing the law. He wasn't the first president to say this. Lyndon B. Johnson and Richard Nixon were also known as law-and-order presidents.

Facing the Facts

There are three branches of the U.S. government. In addition to the executive branch, the legislative branch makes new laws, and the judicial branch **interprets** the law.

In 1965, President Lyndon B. Johnson announced that he was starting a "War on Crime." This meant he wanted to lower crime rates. In 1971, Richard Nixon announced a "War on Drugs." He wanted to lower rates of drug use and crimes related to drugs.

President Lyndon B. Johnson

President Richard Nixon

Being Vague

Most people believe that we should support law and order. They agree that crime is bad and that people should feel safe where they live. However, not everyone agrees on the best way to fight crime and punish criminals. This can lead to confusion, and sometimes people get into arguments about it.

"Law and order" is a very **vague** thing to say. It means different things to different people. When a candidate says they support law and order, one person might think it means they support hiring more police officers. Another person might think it means they support making the prison system better.

Facing the Facts 🔍

In 2005, the United States had about 11,000 Border Patrol officials guarding U.S. borders. Because of fears about border safety, that number had gone up to about 20,000 in 2019.

Law enforcement officers play an important part in the system of law and order.

More Police Power

To some people, supporting law and order means giving more power to the people who enforce the laws. People with this view often think the police should be able to do whatever it takes to stop criminals. They say that if we want law and order, we have to make it harder for criminals to get away.

Laws have been passed to give police and other law enforcement officials more power. Some people think this is a good thing. Other people think that instead of being good for communities, these laws have made the police too powerful.

Facing the Facts

A law known as "stop-and-frisk" gives police the power to stop people on the street and search them to see if they're carrying anything illegal. **Research** has shown that police stop and frisk people of color more than white people.

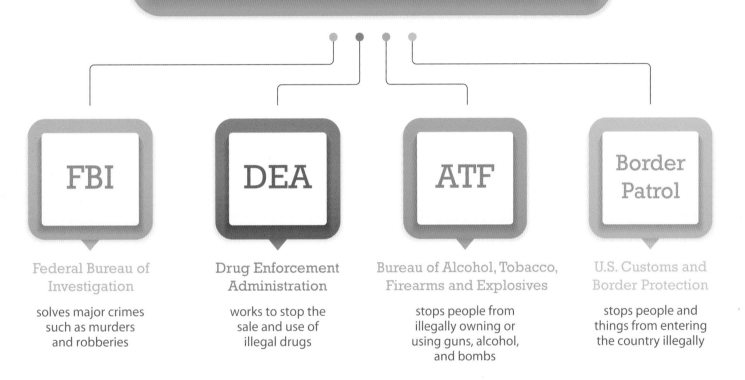

Law Enforcement Agencies

FBI

Federal Bureau of Investigation

solves major crimes such as murders and robberies

DEA

Drug Enforcement Administration

works to stop the sale and use of illegal drugs

ATF

Bureau of Alcohol, Tobacco, Firearms and Explosives

stops people from illegally owning or using guns, alcohol, and bombs

Border Patrol

U.S. Customs and Border Protection

stops people and things from entering the country illegally

There are many different law enforcement groups, or agencies, in the United States. Shown here are some of the biggest ones.

More Accountability

Some people think giving too much importance to the idea of law and order can be a bad thing. They believe too much power can make it easy for law enforcement officers to fail to respect people's rights.

In addition, people who have this view are often worried about police **violence**, also called police brutality. Police officers work to keep people safe, but sometimes a police officer might hurt or even kill someone when they're trying to arrest them. People want police officers to be accountable for their actions. They believe this will help make communities safer.

Facing the Facts

In the United States, Native Americans are more likely to be **victims** of police brutality than any other race.

Most police officers keep people safe, but some police officers have acted in ways that have harmed and even killed people. Many people want those officers to be held accountable for their actions.

Does Prison Work?

The leaders of many state, city, and town governments believe that supporting law and order means arresting more people and putting them in prison. Some people think putting criminals in prison does two good things: It gives them a punishment, and it stops them from committing more crimes.

However, many researchers say that putting a lot of people in prison often leads to more crime, not less. For example, when someone goes to prison, their family might have a harder time paying for things. This might lead the prisoner's family members to try to steal things they can sell to get more money.

Facing the Facts

People who have dealt with **incarceration** often end up in jail again for other crimes. Many people believe better services, such as education, are needed to stop this.

To many people, "law and order" means putting more people in prison. However, research has shown this isn't the best way to decrease crime rates.

Fears About Immigration

Immigration is often part of debates, or arguments, about law and order. President Donald Trump promised to improve law and order in the United States by changing immigration laws. He said he wanted to make sure no criminals were coming into the country.

However, not everyone agreed with Trump that the old immigration laws weren't good enough. They said most immigrants weren't criminals in the first place. Some people worried that instead of being good for law and order, these new immigration laws made it harder for people to leave unsafe countries and come to the United States.

Facing the Facts

Research has shown that crime rates are lower in areas where a lot of immigrants live.

18

Some people liked President Trump's idea to build a wall between the United States and Mexico to keep out criminals. Other people argued there's already a wall (shown here) in many places along the border.

Different Interpretations

People interpret the idea of law and order in many different ways. The way it's interpreted has an effect on the laws people try to pass and how those laws are enforced. Sometimes the laws help, and crime rates go down. Other times, people interpret law and order and act on those interpretations in ways that make crime rates go up.

Law and order can be a very confusing idea, but don't let that stop you from trying to understand it! It's important to know how your leaders interpret it. Then, you can tell them if you agree or disagree with what they're doing to improve law and order.

Facing the Facts

Crime rates have been going down in the United States for years. However, because of the way the news talks about crime, most people think it's been going up.

WHAT CAN YOU DO?

Learn about how the criminal justice system works.

Write to your leaders to tell them if you support or oppose the laws they're passing.

Encourage your parents to vote for candidates who interpret law and order in a way your family agrees with.

If you see anyone committing a crime, report it to your local police station.

Follow the law, and encourage your friends to do the same.

There are many things you can do to help improve law and order in your community!

GLOSSARY

candidate: A person who runs in an election.

commit: To do something—often something that is wrong.

complicated: Difficult to explain or understand.

encourage: To make someone more likely to do something.

enforce: To make sure people do what is required by a rule or law.

immigration: The act of coming to a country to settle there.

incarceration: Holding someone prisoner.

interpret: To explain or understand the meaning of something.

minor: Not as serious or important.

punish: To make someone suffer for doing something wrong.

research: Careful study that is done to find and report new knowledge about something.

tough: Very strict, firm, or determined.

vague: Stated in a way that is general and not clear or precise.

victim: Someone who has been harmed by an unpleasant event.

violence: The use of force to harm someone.

FOR MORE INFORMATION

WEBSITES

BrainPOP: Branches of Government

www.brainpop.com/socialstudies/usgovernment/branchesofgovernment

Through videos, games, and quizzes, this website explains the duties of each branch of government in keeping law and order.

Law for Kids

lawforkids.org

This website, maintained by the Arizona Bar Association, explains laws in a way kids can understand.

BOOKS

Johnson, C. M. *Law Enforcement*. Fremont, CA: Full Tilt Press, 2017.

Keegan, Anna. *The United States Constitution and the Bill of Rights: The Law of the Land*. New York, NY: PowerKids Press, 2016.

Lewis, Daniel. *Public Safety & Law*. Broomall, PA: Mason Crest, 2019.

Publisher's note to educators and parents: Our editors have carefully reviewed these websites to ensure that they are suitable for students. Many websites change frequently, however, and we cannot guarantee that a site's future contents will continue to meet our high standards of quality and educational value. Be advised that students should be closely supervised whenever they access the Internet.

INDEX